LOVE

First published by Parragon in 2011

Parragon
Queen Street House
4 Queen Street
Bath BA1 1HE, UK

www.parragon.com

Copyright © Parragon Books Ltd 2011
Design by Pink Creative Ltd

ISBN: 978-1-4454-4342-3

Printed in China

A special gift from me to you

Bath · New York · Singapore · Hong Kong · Cologne · Delhi
Melbourne · Amsterdam · Johannesburg · Auckland · Shenzhen

Eventually you will come to understand

that love heals everything,

and love is all there is.

5

The best thing about me is you.

Shannon Crown

Life without
love is like
a harp without
strings.

Anonymous

When I first saw you I was afraid to meet you.

When I first met you I was afraid to kiss you.

When I first kissed you I was afraid to love you but now that I love you I'm afraid to lose you.

Anonymous

It's **beauty** that captures your attention; but **personality** that captures your heart.

Anonymous

My favorite place to be is inside of your hugs where it's warm and loving.

Anonymous

15

It's **not** being in love that makes me **happy**. It's **being** in love with you that makes me **happy**.

Anonymous

17

Paradise

is always where

love dwells.

Jean Paul F. Richter

The **best** thing to **hold** onto in life is **each** other.

Audrey Hepburn

A **heart** that loves
is always **young**.

Greek Proverb

Just when I think that
it is impossible
to love you any more,
you prove me wrong.

Anonymous

24

My love for you
is a journey;
Starting at forever,
And ending at never.

Anonymous

27

Let's commit the
perfect crime,
I'll steal your heart
and you'll steal mine.

Anonymous

No man is worth your tears,

and when you find the man who is,

he'll never make you cry.

Anonymous

Without you, I have nothing.
But with you, I have everything.

Anonymous

Where there is great love there are always miracles.

Willa Cather

To the world you

are one person,

but to one person

you are the world.

Anonymous

If a hug represented

how much I loved you,

I would hold you

in my arms forever.

Anonymous

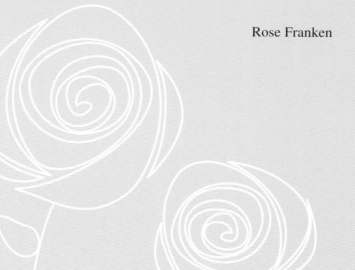

Anyone can be passionate,
but it takes real lovers to be silly.

Rose Franken

I want to be in your arms,

where you hold me tight

and never let me go.

Anonymous

Without his love

I can do nothing,

with his love there is

nothing I cannot do.

Anonymous

Do all things
with love.

Og Mandino

Love isn't something you find. Love is something that finds you.

Loretta Young

Sometimes all I need is a loving hand to hold and a caring heart to understand.

Anonymous

We sat side by side
in the morning light
and looked out at the
future together.

Brian Andres

You know you're in love

when you can't fall asleep because reality is finally better than your dreams.

Dr. Seuss

Only when you  **mix** love and laughter will you get a 'Happily Ever After'.

Anonymous

Whatever our **souls** are made of,

his and mine are the same.

Brontë

Love is

being stupid

together.

Paul Valéry

Love puts the

fun in together,

the **sad** in apart,

and the **joy** in a heart.

Anonymous

The **best** portion of a good man's life is the little, nameless, unremembered acts of **kindness** and **love**.

William Wordsworth

Grow old along with me
the best is yet to be.

Robert Browning

I'm so in love,

every time I look at you

my soul gets dizzy.

Jesse Tyler

Where there is love there is life.

Indira Gandhi

If I know what love is,

it is because of you.

Herman Hesse

I love you, not for what you are,
but for what I am when I am with you.

Roy Croft

Anyone can catch your eye,
but it takes someone special
to catch your heart.

Anonymous

When I see you, the world stops as if the only purpose in life was for me to please you.

Anonymous

As long as you hold me,
I am safe from all harm.

Anonymous

Love looks not with the eyes, but with the mind; and therefore is winged Cupid painted blind.

William Shakespeare

A hundred hearts would be too few.

To carry all my love for you.

Anonymous

Soul meets soul on
lovers' lips.

Percy Bysshe Shelley

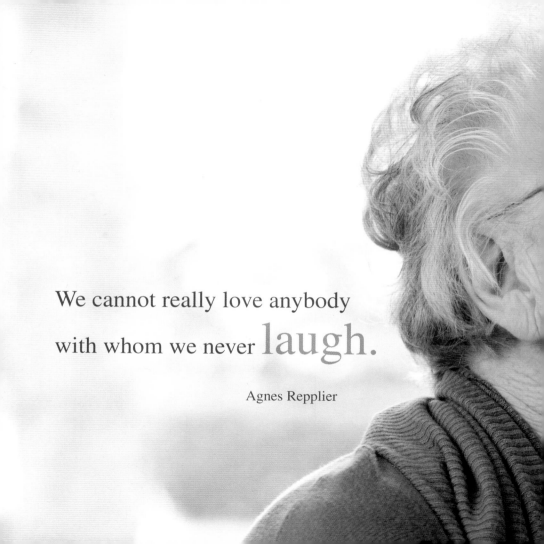

We cannot really love anybody
with whom we never laugh.

Agnes Repplier

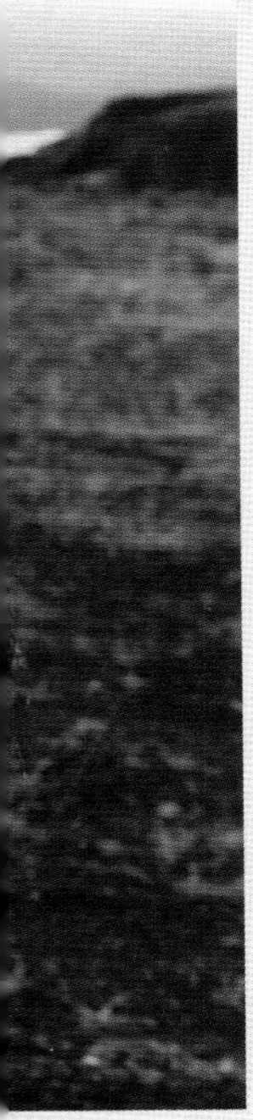

You don't marry
someone you can live with
—you marry the person who
you cannot live without.

Anonymous

Now join your hands,

and with your hands

your hearts.

William Shakespeare

All you **need** is love.

John Lennon

Picture credits

P4-5 © Christopher Wurzbach/Getty; p6-7 © B. Blue/Getty; p8-9 © David De Lossy/Getty; p10-11 © Marcy Maloy/Getty; p12-13 © Rolf Bruderer/Getty; p14-15 © Marcus Lund/Getty; p16-17 © Thomas Barwick/Getty; p18-19 Sri Maiava Rusden/Getty; p20-21 © Chris Ted/Getty; p22-23 © Sollina Images/Getty; p24-25 © Tom Merton/Getty; p26-27 © Cultura/Getty; p28-29 © JonPaul Douglass/Getty; p30-31 © kevinruss/Getty; p32-33 © Madeleine Stevens/Getty; p34-35 © Thomas Barwick/Getty; p36-37 © rubberball/Getty; p38-39 © Plush Studios/Getty;p40-41 © Dragan Todorovic/Getty; p42-43 © Thomas Barwick/Getty; p44-45 © Walter Sanders/Getty; p46-47 © Thomas Barwick; p48-49 © DreamPictures/Getty; p50-51 © Lauri Rotko/Getty; p52-53 © Reggie Casagrande/Getty; p54-55 © Lauri Rotko/Getty; p56-57 © Ojo Images/Getty; p58-59 © Priscilla Gragg/Getty; p60-61 © Cultura/Zero Creatives/Getty; p62-63 © Karan Kapoor/Getty; p64-65 © Bree Walk/Getty; p66-67 © Peter Cade/Getty; p68-69 © Cavan Images/Getty; p70-71 © Cavan Images/Getty; p72-73 © Adam Burn/Getty; p74-75 © ack Hollingsworth/Getty; p76-77 © Dennis Hallinan/Getty; p78-79 © Rolf Bruderer/Getty; p80-81 © Betsie van der Meer/Getty; p82-83 © momentimages/Getty; p84-85 © David H. Collier/Getty; p86-87 © momentimages/Getty; p88-89 Paul Burns/Getty; p90-91 © Thomas Barwick/Getty; p92-93 © Philip and Karen Smith/Getty; p94-95 © GAP Photos/Getty.